Scotland

Edited By Kat Cockrill

First published in Great Britain in 2019 by:

Young Writers
Remus House
Coltsfoot Drive
Peterborough
PE2 9BF
Telephone: 01733 890066
Website: www.youngwriters.co.uk

All Rights Reserved
Book Design by Ashley Janson
© Copyright Contributors 2019
Softback ISBN 978-1-78988-893-5
Hardback ISBN 978-1-83928-456-4
Printed and bound in the UK by BookPrintingUK
Website: www.bookprintinguk.com
YB0418A

FOREWORD

Welcome Reader, to a world of dreams.

For Young Writers' latest competition, we asked our writers to dig deep into their imagination and create a poem that paints a picture of what they dream of, whether it's a make-believe world full of wonder or their aspirations for the future.

The result is this collection of fantastic poetic verse that covers a whole host of different topics. Let your mind fly away with the fairies to explore the sweet joy of candy lands, join in with a game of fantasy football, or you may even catch a glimpse of a unicorn or another mythical creature. Beware though, because even dreamland has dark corners, so you may turn a page and walk into a nightmare!

Whereas the majority of our writers chose to stick to a free verse style, others gave themselves the challenge of other techniques such as acrostics and rhyming couplets. We also gave the writers the option to compose their ideas in a story, so watch out for those narrative pieces too!

Each piece in this collection shows the writers' dedication and imagination – we truly believe that seeing their work in print gives them a well-deserved boost of pride, and inspires them to keep writing, so we hope to see more of their work in the future!

CONTENTS

Independent Entries

B Stevenson (10) — 1

All Saints Primary School, Airdrie

Katie Smart (9) — 2
Mischa Brown (9) — 4
Cara Mortimer (10) — 6
Ava Mina (9) — 7
Matthew Thomas Harrison (10) — 8
Orin Neish (9) — 9
Gemma Kelly (9) — 10
Alexander O'Hanlon (9) — 11
Neve Allan (9) — 12
Hannah Dearie (9) — 13

Bankier Primary School, Banknock

Calum Thomas McFarlane (10) — 14
Sofia Annette Boyle (9) — 15
Taliah Omand (9) — 16
Memphis Walker (9) — 17
Lewis Robertson (10) — 18
Jessica Donnelly (10) — 19
Chloe Fitzpatrick (9) — 20
Katy Sherry (10) — 21
Deena Collins (9) — 22
Niamh Charlotte Malone (9) — 23
Peter William James Hutchison (9) — 24
Josh Connell (9) — 25

Bridge Of Weir Primary School, Bridge Of Weir

Connie McLeod (10) — 26
Owen Mackay (10) — 27
Jack Colin Cook (11) — 28
William Singer (11) — 29
Sofia Kishore (11) — 30
Casey Addison-Lyle — 31
Andrea Coyle (11) — 32
Katie Stevenson (10) — 33
Ben Provan (10) — 34
Daniel Lawler (11) — 35
Lucy Rankin (10) — 36
Jamie Stewart — 37
Michael Sanders (11) — 38
Sean Skilling (10) — 39
Daisy Adams (11) — 40
Cait Forbes (11) — 41

Flora Stevenson Primary School, Edinburgh

Scarlett Leonard (10) — 42
Lola Clark (11) — 44
Alexander Macleod (11) — 45
Sophia Elaine McRae-Ellis (10) — 46
Tristan Wake (11) — 47
Donald MacBeath (10) — 48
Pratheesa Minnal Sathish (11) — 49
Natalia Stolarz Szeremeta (10) — 50
Zoë Viale (10) — 51
Iris Dagg (10) — 52
Cara Taylor (10) — 53
William Turner (11) — 54
James Behan (11) — 55

Ayusma Kunwar (10)	56
Bea Murray (10)	57
Max Cleland (10)	58
Stella Smith (10)	59
Cameron Boyd (11)	60

Golfhill Primary School, Airdrie

Katie Loudon (9)	61
Mirryn McCormick (9)	62
Eilidh Mcginness (9)	63
Ellie Easton (10)	64
Caleb Hamill (9)	65
John Moultrie (9)	66
Isla Kerr (10)	67
Aaron Alexander Fraser (9)	68
Erin McLaughlin (9)	69
Jack Graham Cunningham (10)	70
Sophie Hughes (10)	71
Hassan Ayub (9)	72
Lewis Vance (9)	73
Keira Brown (10)	74
Rory Anderson (9)	75
Lauren Robertson (10)	76
Jack Grant (9)	77
Lewis Anderson (9)	78
Noah Magennis (9)	79
Lucy Marshall (10)	80
Caleb Young (10)	81
Cole Ferguson (9)	82
Ava Keenan (9)	83

Heriot Primary School, Paisley

John Keenan (10)	84
Ellie Louise McLaren (10)	85
James Hunter (10)	86
Alex Reekie (10)	87
Riley Meechan (11)	88
Jamie James McKechnie (11)	89
Morgan Gallacher (11)	90
Rory Young (10)	91
Keira Abbie (10)	92
Kenzie Milne (10)	93

Hannah McCallum (10)	94
Sophie Karen Help (11)	95
Marcus Issac (10)	96
Amber McKinnon (10)	97

Hillside School, Portlethen

Liliana Biros (7)	98
Emma Miller (7)	99
Inioluwa Adejugba (7)	100
Megan Lucy Kenyon (7)	101
Hannah Milne (7)	102
Shyloh Duncan (8)	103
Olivia Abbey Davie (8)	104
Lewis Tawse (7)	105
Keira Jackson (7)	106
Ashrith Padakanti (7)	107
Elvita Srivastava (7)	108
Harriet Conner (7)	109
Indy Hunter (7)	110
Amy Mitchell (8)	111
Emmie Milne (8)	112
Mason McRobb (8)	113
Cameron Tempest (7)	114
Aston Pender (8)	115
Chimzara Victor Roberts (7)	116
Jamie Moncur (8)	117
Emma Lewis (7)	118
Ella Milne (7)	119
Olivia Milne (8)	120
Abbie Pirie (7)	121
Harry Auld (8)	122
Ryan Weng (8)	123
Jessica Ellie Robertson (8)	124
Komeno Jaden Obaruakporo (7)	125
Ruby Walker (7)	126
Daniel Robert Murray (8)	127
Ife Adeyemi (7)	128
Flynn Taylor (7)	129
Campbell Stephen (7)	130
Dara Shadare (8)	131
Leah Kemp (7)	132
Lewis Michie (7)	133
Maddisyn McInnes (7)	134

Mason John Gill (7)	135
Maisie Ruby Fraser (7)	136
Cooper Inglis (7)	137
Nathan Laing (7)	138
Devin Cameron (7)	139
Chloe South (8)	140

Kilchattan Primary School, Kilchattan

Felix Musgrave-Dance (9)	141
Rosie Musgrave-Dance (10)	142
Eve Liddell (9)	144
Eleanor Grieve (9)	145

Knowetop Primary School, Motherwell

Jessica Mitchell (8)	146
Isla Kennedy (8)	148
Francesca Muir (8)	150
Fizah Arshad Nawaz (9)	151
Maisie Watters (8)	152
Cameron Angus Hill (8)	154
Daniel Fiddes (8)	155
Ross Mitchell (7)	156
Marc McGill (9)	157
Aaron Gribbon (7)	158
Sophie Cowie (8)	159
Harry Greve (8)	160
Olivia Picken (8)	161
Matthew Pettigrew (9)	162
Callum Johnstone (8)	163
Cameron David McFarlane (7)	164
Harry Jenkins (8)	165
Calum Preston (8)	166
Cameron Mills Begley (7)	167
Luke Craig (7)	168

St Vincent's Primary School, Carnwadric

Damaris Asuquo (11)	169

Strathpeffer Primary School, Strathpeffer

Connie Mackain (11)	171
Evie Hallam (11)	172
Orrin Stirling-Guy (11)	173
Daniel Hallam (11)	174

Whinhill Primary School, Greenock

Ethan James Bennett (8)	175
Lisa Gillen (8)	176
Emily Ruth Humphreys (9)	177
Eilidh MacNab (8)	178
Brooke Dickson (8)	179
Taylor Dickson (8)	180
Ethan McIntosh (8)	181
Ava Young (8)	182
Abigail Eva Milligan (8)	183
Kyle Duncan Thompson (8)	184
Olivia Logsdon (9)	185
Mia Gorman (8)	186
Cameron Kelly (8)	187
Lochlainn Dale (8)	188
Nicholas Robertson (8)	189
Paige Louisa McLennan (8)	190

THE POEMS

Candy Land

C ats and rainbow bunnies are my company
A nd my rainbow dogs and unicorn,
N ear the house, I find a magic key,
D ogs are in funny costumes and I went through a magic portal,
Y eah! I saw a rainbow smiling at me!

L ollipops are there, waving at me,
A stronauts are waving their cheery feet at me,
N ever-ending river of white chocolate,
D riving marshmallows are clapping happily today in my dreams.

B Stevenson (10)

Once Upon A Dream

As I slowly drifted off to sleep, I closed my eyes and I saw my friends around me. There were fruity, sweet scents floating in the breeze, the fluffy rainbow clouds floated around the sky and there were fairies dancing on the ground. I rose to my feet and followed my friends for they were walking to where the dream would end.

We continued to walk until we saw butterflies and sweets, I jumped into a lake filled with cake. Then everything in my dream turned dark and I no longer enjoyed it. Something was glowing up ahead. I didn't think I wanted to go any longer for the sky was grey and the mood was sombre. I enjoyed it before but I wanted to turn back. I tried to run away but I could not turn back, a wall covered where we were.

I turned back around and my friends were gone like the wind, they were gone! I did not know what to do, I was lost in something that was not a dream, it was a nightmare.

I felt upset but I soon found out that all the unicorns had lost their magic. I would have to go and look for the magic that had been stolen by the rogue fairies.

I thought I saw some fairies with some extra powers doing things that fairies shouldn't have been able to do. I tried to catch them but they moved too fast.

What was that horrible noise? It sounded like an alarm! My alarm for school! So, it was all just a dream. Oh well, what a shame that I couldn't see the rest of the dream. I wonder where I will be the next time I dream?

Katie Smart (9)
All Saints Primary School, Airdrie

Once Upon A Dream

On a nice warm night in the middle of June,
In the light of the moon,
Was Emirates stadium.
I was watching basketball, all my friends were there,
The UK mascot was giving freebies chair to chair,
Today was a very happy day,
UK beat the other country,
But then, the Emirates' owner said,
"I am closing Emirates down..."
My dad did not like the sound of that,
He started to think as he sat,
Then he went to the owner and said,
"Why are you closing it down?"
He replied, "This place is haunted, can't you see?
But if you want to fix it, you can get it for free!
Do you want it?" The owner asked.
Dad said, "I just might!"
I was filled with delight,
But, living there was a nightmare!

  N othing good about it,
   I couldn't bear it,
  G osh, this is so bad,
  H elp me, someone,

T otally a bad idea,
M an, this is awful,
A bad choice,
R eally weird,
E verything is bad.

I got lost one million times. Mum said I was melodramatic,
But, somehow, I got stuck in the attic,
I am so annoyed, my mum said I would be fine,
But life is not that divine,
I was about to scream
But then I realised it was once upon a dream!

Mischa Brown (9)
All Saints Primary School, Airdrie

King Nightmare And Wishland

Once upon a dream, I woke up with my coconut-coloured chow-chow Bailey jumping all over me. She looked happy that I was awake. "Okay, okay! I'll get up!" She got off me finally.
Slowly but surely, I got off the grass. "Where am I?" I wondered. Everything was rainbow, the grass, water, trees, clouds, sky, even the sun was rainbow! "What? I wish I knew where I was!" I mumbled out loud.
Suddenly, a letter was in my hand. It said, 'You are in Wish Land!' Confused, I said, "I wish I was rich!" Suddenly, I was rich.
This went on for hours. Bailey was rich too until soon it had to end and it turned pitch-black. "Bailey? Where are you?" I started to shout, louder and louder. I woke up in a black and grey world, just like the rainbow world but black and grey. "Bailey!" I shouted as Bailey jumped on me.
I heard a voice behind me. "I'm King Nightmare, I will take you and your dog to my chamber of sin!"
Next, I woke up in the chamber, stuck to a chair with Bailey strapped to me. I tried to escape, then all the walls started to cave in. Then they stopped and I was back in Rainbow Land.

Cara Mortimer (10)
All Saints Primary School, Airdrie

An Unknown Land

I had woken up somewhere that I hadn't ever been before, my legs in the water. That's when I realised I was on the seashore. I wandered and wandered in the wood, very frightened, I put up my hood.
The sound of food boiling in the pan, I followed the noise, I thought I should, but as I got closer, it sounded no good. I noticed a large waterfall, but then I noticed quite a small wall. Beside the wall was a door which led to a strange-shaped hall.
The waterfall sucked me in, I was panicking so I started to swim. I woke up on the other side, it was a lot bigger and very wide. I looked to the ground and got a fright, then turned around to something bright. It took a while to figure out what creatures were about, this wasn't a normal creature. It was pale white and its eyes were shining bright, that's how I knew it was a creature of the night.
As it scooped me up with its beautiful wings, it showed me extremely cool things.
I woke up fast, with a scream, that's when I noticed it was a dream.

Ava Mina (9)
All Saints Primary School, Airdrie

Once Upon A Dream

Once upon a time, on a gloomy day in a gloomy swamp, *bang!* An old witch was hatching a plan, with a little bit of this and a little bit of that. The sky turned black and the wicked witch spoke in a crackly voice. She said, "Beware of the terrible things I may bring!" As the sky boomed and she flew around the black night sky, the wicked witch gave everyone a fright, except for her black cat of course.

When the king heard about this, he started his daring plan. It wasn't an easy plan, it took days upon days to finish. He held a party for the plan, but did he know about the witch's plan?

When she heard about the party, she took action and she made three potions which she took to the sky and she said, "Fly high!" followed by a creepy cackle, but then her cat fell, then she fell, then she fell flat on her face in cake, and then she ran and ran to her heart's content. The guards chased her, but she was never found again.

Matthew Thomas Harrison (10)
All Saints Primary School, Airdrie

The Magic Mermaid

Once upon a dream, there were three girls called Orin, Mya and Gabrielle. The girls were out on a boat trip, it was dark and stormy. Gabrielle was steering the ship while Orin and Mya fell asleep. Ten minutes later, Mya woke up and saw a mermaid steering the ship. She walked up to the mermaid and said, "Who are you?" The mermaid replied, "I'm Merry, who are you?"
Mya said, "I'm Mya, nice to meet you!"
Orin and Gabrielle woke up and ate lunch. Merry had a salad, Orin and Gabrielle had some shrimp and Mya had a banana and Nutella wrap. Merry was upset because Orin and Gabrielle were eating her sea friends. Orin and Gabrielle both said, with joy, "Mmm, that was delicious!" They were playing tig, but Merry couldn't because of her mermaid tail. An hour later, the girls fell asleep. Orin woke up in her bedroom and said, "Was it a dream all along?"

Orin Neish (9)
All Saints Primary School, Airdrie

Dream Land

During the night, I dreamed of a land
with rainbows and unicorns and sparkly sand.
Everywhere I looked there were magical creatures
and fast-flying dragons with scary-looking features.
My favourite sight was a really tiny house.
Large and big creatures and some the size of a mouse.
All the animals were happy and dancing,
nothing was as strange as a frog who was prancing.
Dogs were jumping and rabbits were walking,
monkeys and owls were excitedly talking.
I looked up to the sky and I could see
a giant, cheeky monkey flying over me.
Inside one of the houses, I could hear
a calm little bunny with no fear.
Sunshine started to get bright,
then I saw a dragon in flight and I got a big fright.
Now it is morning, the minutes felt so quick.
It was such a lovely dream, the best dream ever,
I really wish it ended never!

Gemma Kelly (9)
All Saints Primary School, Airdrie

The Helicoprin

Having a birthday is the best thing you can get because you have so much fun and you get lots of presents and delicious cake, but the worst of all is waiting for everyone to come and having to take pictures. So, my full family and a couple of my friends were at Deep Sea World for my birthday. I could get anything, so I picked a shark, an extinct one as well. It was a Helicoprin and we were all going to see it with a lot more sharks and fish.

One hour later, there was lots of screaming. *Bash! Bash!* We all went down. It was the Helicoprin, there was water everywhere, people were swimming for their lives, dead people were on and in the water. It was freaky but we all made it but then we noticed the shark and the water was rising.

"Wake up!"

My bed was wet and I was hugging my toy shark. Was it a dream?

Alexander O'Hanlon (9)
All Saints Primary School, Airdrie

The Magical Dragon

Once upon a dream, I was sitting on the couch. My mum was reading my report card and, since it was good, my mum said we could go shopping. When we went shopping, I went around the whole toy store but, finally, I saw a toy dragon! It was so cute, so I got it (but my mum bought it). When we got home, I went upstairs to my room, I sat down with it. It said something on the label, so I rubbed it and the dragon came alive and it was life-sized!
I asked the dragon why he was here and he whispered in my ear, "Come with me and you will see a world of imagination!" I was shocked and then he picked me up and then we flew out the window and flew all around the world! When I got home, the dragon tucked me into bed and I realised it was all a dream!

Neve Allan (9)
All Saints Primary School, Airdrie

Once Upon A Dream

One day, I was walking my dog and I saw a big, gloomy tree with a door, so I thought that maybe I could go in. When I went in, I got transported to another dimension. It looked the same but I knew something was wrong from the way I travelled there. One moment later, my dog started barking. I looked behind me and saw a unicorn with a golden horn and then a dark black unicorn. I walked back and then I ran away to the portal but it was gone. Then I felt something nudging me but then I woke up to my room. Wait, was that a dream?

Hannah Dearie (9)
All Saints Primary School, Airdrie

Pokémon: Shadows Unite

Tonight, I didn't want to go to sleep,
So I stood up and went to count sheep,
Then I couldn't stay up and went to sleep in a second,
When I got up, I looked around and thought that I was in heaven,
I went in and looked around and thought it was fab,
I walked to a cave and heard a sound,
Then I looked around and couldn't believe what I found,
A Pokémon as yellow as can be,
I went in the cave but didn't see,
Then the Pokémon guided me,
The brightness in its fur,
Then I had to fight whoever,
Send out a Pokémon who was taller,
I got a black Pokémon, wow!
The coldness made me shiver!
I battled hard with all my strength,
So I sent out a pink Pokémon and what a length!
I soon battled and battled until I won,
Then I knew I was done.

Calum Thomas McFarlane (10)
Bankier Primary School, Banknock

Space Dream

I slowly open my eyes and I'm floating in space,
I see planets and stars all over the place,
Earth, Mercury, Venus and Saturn,
All wondering how this actually happened?

I hear lots of talking but from where?
"Who's that girl?" said something over there,
I turn around and scream, for what I see
Earth is the one talking to me!

I spin around and all the planets are here,
I think the sun must be near,
The moon is here with a smile on his face,
The stars that are dancing challenge me to a race!

I am very confused at this magical world,
I watch as all the planets twirled,
I then looked down and I was in my bed,
Woke up in the morning, wondering what just happened in my head!

Sofia Annette Boyle (9)
Bankier Primary School, Banknock

A Magical Dream

This magical dream all started last night,
Something tapped my back and I screamed, "You really gave me a fright!"
"Oh, I'm so sorry!" replied Star,
"I just wanted to ask if you would like a delicious unicorn fizz bar?"
"Sure," I replied, "but could you show me around?"
"Yes!" said the unicorn, replying with a bound,
"Thanks!" I said. "But what was that sound?"
"Oh, it's just Poppy, the magic fairy, she's so kind!"
All the fun ideas swirled in my mind,
But, before I knew it, there was a flash,
I woke up hearing my mum whispering,
"Sit up and eat your baked beans and mash!"

Taliah Omand (9)
Bankier Primary School, Banknock

The Dream Jar

Last night, when I was going to bed,
I wrote a dream for my jar,
I put it in, I shook it
And I hoped it would happen.

I shut my eyes,
An adventure was waiting,
After a flash, my mind was racing!
After a bang, my dreams got mixed up,
When I noticed it was my jar
I was too lazy to get that far.

One of my dreams was to see a flying alpaca,
Making a noise, she was holding maracas!
She flew me to where my next dream would be!

My biggest dream yet was to see a castle,
The alpaca took me without hassle,
When I woke up, I was in my bed,
All of my dreams went out of my head!

Memphis Walker (9)
Bankier Primary School, Banknock

Mythical Creatures!

Opening portals, opening doors,
What will be inside? What will be there?
Jumping in with my friend,
What will I create?
Dark monsters, mythical creatures,
Metro cities, dark wars,
Losing, losing, winning, winning,
Battle within growing,
Members losing members,
What shall I do?
New friends in the real world,
Jumping back in the portal,
Growing, fighting,
Sea creatures!
We all prepared for war,
During the war, I suddenly felt dizzy,
I opened my eyes, what a dream!

Lewis Robertson (10)
Bankier Primary School, Banknock

A Dream

D ays and days went past and then this happened,
R ight there, that night, I was in a dream,
E veryone was pink and white,
A rgh! I got a fright,
M y heart was beating so fast,
S o I ran for my life.

O h my, they are fast!
F or my safety, I ran like The Flash.

L et me hide,
I will be safe,
F inally, I woke up and I fell out of bed,
E verything was normal!

Jessica Donnelly (10)
Bankier Primary School, Banknock

Lots And Lots Of Dreams In My Head!

Last night, in bed,
A dream scattered in my head,
I was brought to a magical place,
But then it turned out I was in a race!
I ran and ran but still came last,
But, finally, I ran really fast,
I won the race at a good pace
And I had a big smile on my face!

I once had another dream
That I went in a magical beam!
I was teleported to another dreamland
And I played in a band!

Chloe Fitzpatrick (9)
Bankier Primary School, Banknock

My Dream Job

Last night, when I went to bed,
A dream started in my head,
I was a runner in a race,
To beat all the others' pace,
When I got my medal, I had a big, happy face,
I ran and ran as fast as I could,
'Til I was a winner, it was good.

Then, a flying llama came
And took me to another race,
It was a blast
Like a trip to the past.

Katy Sherry (10)
Bankier Primary School, Banknock

Nightmare Dream

Come back, my clown,
I couldn't see you last night,
I went through bad things to steal your nose,
Help me, help me, little clown,
I couldn't stop laughing about your red hair and nose,
Come on, my friend,
Tell me a joke,
You're like my lovely snowball,
I love you so much,
Shut your eyes,
There are sparkles all over your eyes.

Deena Collins (9)
Bankier Primary School, Banknock

Killer Dream

Nothing happened 'til that night, when I went to bed,
A scary dream popped into my head,
I was a spy but I was not shy,
Then I saw a killer who could fly,
There he was, floating in the sky.

A flash of lightning in the midnight sky,
There was a killer, beneath my eyes,
In a flash of my eye, I could fly,
I thought I would die.

Niamh Charlotte Malone (9)
Bankier Primary School, Banknock

The Fortnite Win

I was in a game
With no one to blame,
A gun popped,
I nearly dropped,
Gunfire, rapid-fire,
With a wolf named Dire,
In Mosley Mire,
New mega-mall,
I don't like it at all,
'Cause I always fall,
Snake in the cake
With high stakes,
That is all I take!

Peter William James Hutchison (9)
Bankier Primary School, Banknock

I Am A Superhero

I am a superhero, swinging through the city,
Fighting crime wherever I go,
I meet new villains on the way,
They just keep coming back, they won't go away!
There are so many
And I don't know where to start,
Then I crashed into a building
Where somebody was fishing!

Josh Connell (9)
Bankier Primary School, Banknock

The Howl

Once upon a time, in a land far away,
I was looking into the eyes of my prey,
It was big, it was brown,
It was hairy and fowl,
It was what you call a Howl.

A Howl is a creature
That has big, wide open eyes
And their nose is like a human's,
Their ears are big and furry
And they smell like curry
And if you can't guess, their howl can deafen you!

As the Howl approached, I made my move,
I took a step forward
And, as soon as I did, the Howl howled,
I screamed as loud as a werewolf,
I felt myself shaking, so I opened my eyes
And realised it was all a dream.

Connie McLeod (10)
Bridge Of Weir Primary School, Bridge Of Weir

The Forest, The House And The Armour

Once, long ago,
In a forest far away,
A boy was strolling through.
The ground was like rock
And the trees were dancing to the wind's beat.
As the sun rose in the moonlit sky,
The boy spotted a house
With gummy bear walls and candy cane doors.
As he stood in front of it
And knocked and knocked,
He took a look,
But that was all that it took.
He crept in
And looked in the bin
To find an old knight's suit.
He put it on to find himself stuck.
Stuck, no help, nothing.
There he stood, stuck like a lion in a cage,
Hoping to wake up now.

Owen Mackay (10)
Bridge Of Weir Primary School, Bridge Of Weir

Candy Land

In the centre of Candy Land,
A group of deer were wandering
Around the pink fields,
Observing the candyfloss trees,
Huge candy canes stuck in the ground
Were blocking their view of the chocolate castle
Where the king lived,
Birds made of bubblegum flew above them
As two huge buffalo made of candy cane
Walked beside them,
They walked past a river filled with soda,
There was a forest that they could rest in for the warmer months,
So they could stay cool, they decided it was the best place to rest,
They entered and stayed until the heat went down.

Jack Colin Cook (11)
Bridge Of Weir Primary School, Bridge Of Weir

The Boy Who Dreamed Wolf

One night, as dark as day,
The owls flew above the trees like planes above the clouds,
People were sleeping, like Grandad sleeping in his red apple chair,
Then, a howl from a creature, screeching and fearsome,
Awoke a boy from his midnight dream,
The boy got up and went to the door
And peeped out into the dark night,
He leapt and jumped and screamed,
Hairy and deadly, the creature went right in
And asked him to tea,
The boy slapped himself,
Happily finding himself in his crazy bed,
He went downstairs to check it was just a dream.

William Singer (11)
Bridge Of Weir Primary School, Bridge Of Weir

Dream Jars

Once upon a time,
I was stuck in a dream jar,
It was peaceful, like a warm bath,
Sweets dancing in the transparent sky,
Weird but wonderful creatures flew by.

One night, I saw an amazing sight,
Some sort of flight,
A plane or a helicopter,
Inside the plane, there was a creature,
A pink, flower-shaped thing,
It was the Queen Perfume,
The ruler here!
She gracefully flew down and said,
"Wake up!"
I opened my eyes to see my mum,
Telling me that it was time for school.

Sofia Kishore (11)
Bridge Of Weir Primary School, Bridge Of Weir

Your Worst Nightmare!

One day, I woke up
And saw a very unusual creature over there,
What a jump-scare!
Over there was a monster in his underwear!
What a weird sight to see! What?
Now there's three!
Where did they come from?
Oh no, what's that beside them?
Is that, no, it can't be...
A monster with ten dirty eyes with blood all over!
What a giant jump-scare!
It also has very, very long, ugly hair,
One morning, I awoke,
With my dog licking my ear
And I couldn't hear out of that ear.

Casey Addison-Lyle
Bridge Of Weir Primary School, Bridge Of Weir

Once Upon A Dream

O nce I had a dream,
N ow I am a witch,
C an I go to Hogwarts?
E very wizard goes!

U mbridge is gone,
P lease let me use my wand,
O nto spells and potions,
N ow, my wand is as fast as lightning,

A nd *whoosh!* goes my broomstick

D oes McGonagall notice?
R unning to Hagrid's hut,
E normous door to go through,
A little baby dragon
M akes me think I can wake.

Andrea Coyle (11)
Bridge Of Weir Primary School, Bridge Of Weir

The Chef That Was Scared Of Toast!

I went out for dinner,
Wasn't expecting this,
'Cause when I asked the fat chef
What I could have on my shiny silver dish,
"Anything but toast, oh not toast,
It scares me the most!"
"Okay!" I said, with a shivering voice,
Thinking that I had a very big choice,
So, I ordered fish
To go on my shiny silver dish,
Ate all of it and shouted, "Delish!"
Oh no, now it's time for dessert!

Katie Stevenson (10)
Bridge Of Weir Primary School, Bridge Of Weir

Barcelona

B alls running left, right and centre into the goal,
A team with a leader who is as great as a god,
R oar goes the crowd when they score,
C hampions they are with Messi,
E very win is good for every man on the team,
L osing is not an option for them,
O ne thing that is for sure,
N othing will stop this team,
A team called Barcelona that I dream of being in!

Ben Provan (10)
Bridge Of Weir Primary School, Bridge Of Weir

Once Upon A Dream

D aniel Lawler will be a football legend, better than Pele and Maradona,

R onaldo is brilliant but Daniel is better, in strength, skill and finishing,

E ager to shoot, he was unselfish and passed the ball, it soared through the air like a plane,

A lfredo Morelos is such a hack and dives, it's unbelievable!

M o Salah will lead Liverpool to Champions League glory and they will lift the trophy!

Daniel Lawler (11)
Bridge Of Weir Primary School, Bridge Of Weir

Sugar Rush

Doughnut Land is covered in sprinkles,
Glitter rains from the cotton candy clouds,
Wherever you look, sugar is surrounding you,
The glaze from the doughnut gets in your hair,
But, when your teeth fall out
You aren't going to pout,
Your teeth, lying there, as rotten as a rat,
Also, they're as orange as cheesy Wotsits,
You awake from your dream and scream...

Lucy Rankin (10)
Bridge Of Weir Primary School, Bridge Of Weir

Candy Land

There was a house made out of sweets
And the chocolate was like infinite sweets
And it tasted like ice cream
And it smelt like cake with white icing,
Surrounding the lovely Mars sky
Was cotton candy as pink as a flamingo,
The environment was as beautiful as the sunset,
It smelt like a lovely flapjack,
The clouds smelt like candyfloss.

Jamie Stewart
Bridge Of Weir Primary School, Bridge Of Weir

My Dream To Become A Cartoonist

Can I have an art degree
And make this dream a reality?
I will study art and
Not throw a dart
Through my cartoonist dream,
I would love to draw like a master,
In an animation studio,
Drawing creatures,
Real or mythical,
Art is great
So open up your imagination gate!

Michael Sanders (11)
Bridge Of Weir Primary School, Bridge Of Weir

Narnia

N arnia is as cold as ice,
A fter, Aslan came,
"**R** oar!" said the lion,
N o one could stop him, he is the father of the gods,
I wish I could tell him that lions don't speak,
A nd, with lions, I will dream.

Sean Skilling (10)
Bridge Of Weir Primary School, Bridge Of Weir

Dreamland

It's upside down in Dreamland,
The sky is as green as emeralds
And the floor is covered in clouds,
Birds cheep at our feet
Triangular-shaped buses fly above us,
Minuscule purple bears fly planes
Like rocket ships in the night.

Daisy Adams (11)
Bridge Of Weir Primary School, Bridge Of Weir

A Wonderful Cycle

I went for a cycle on my bike,
Round and round my wheels went,
I looked to my left to see,
The beautiful sea full of fish,
Planes glided through the sky,
Like rocket ships in the night.

Cait Forbes (11)
Bridge Of Weir Primary School, Bridge Of Weir

Off The Script

The darkness around me is a shadow of fear,
The thud of footsteps are like drums,
A reflection of fear and mistakes has finally appeared,
The floorboards creak like a mouse
As the door slowly swings open on the rusty hinges,
A fearful creature appears from the dark,
The robotic joints twist and turn as it approaches me,
Teeth like daggers that could easily kill,
Wires hang out of limbs and teeth on every joint,
The other door creaks open as more fearful creatures appear,
They surround the bed where I sit,
Three creatures of death,
One is a nightmarish, robotic fox with a hook like a pirate,
Another a robotic bunny with fearful eyes,
And the last,
The bear, all golden and withered with those sharp teeth,
Creak! go the joints as he moves his head,
His creepy red eyes stare through me,
His teeth so close to my face,
I close my eyes to hope to find a plain, dark room,
With no fears or horrors in sight,

But, when I open my eyes,
The nightmares are still there,
I hope this is all just a dream,
Or am I stuck in a prison of my nightmares?

Scarlett Leonard (10)
Flora Stevenson Primary School, Edinburgh

A Night Of Repeating Horrors

One Friday night, the clock strikes nine,
You go to see if anybody is free,
So you call, you message, but it ends with a tone,
So, you go to see who is home,
Finally, you enter into black night,
It's as dark as a buried bat,
It's cold and the fear shivers up your back,
You enter the show as a firework explodes,
You get a fright but you remember it's fireworks night,
Ever so suddenly, a clown appears,
It disappears then reappears, it's a scary clown fear!
I hear a bang, bang, then cold blood on fingertips
On the edge of my heart,
Shoulder is getting colder,
I turn around to see the evil eyes of a clown
Welcoming me into unknown darkness,
It scares me, it fears me, I get in a muddle,
But then I realise there's nowhere to huddle
At the end of the night,
I get a fright,
I wake up from my dream
And give a loud scream,
Then I remember it's just a dream.

Lola Clark (11)
Flora Stevenson Primary School, Edinburgh

Shrinking

Going to the beach, just a normal, fun day,
Packing our picnic without delay,
When we got to the beach, there was one space left
But the man sitting next to it looked like he'd committed theft,
We set out our things but I was really thirsty,
I saw a bottle but it looked quite dirty,
I drank it all up but announced with shock, "Help!"
I'd shrunk to the size of a Lego brick!
I was ready to panic, but all I could see
Was a huge, scary spider coming to get me,
I started to run with a *thud, thud, thud!*
But the spider caught up and threw me like a piece of crud,
I flew like a bird, I was really happy,
But nothing lasts long when you get hit by toffee,
My brother threw it, of course he did,
He roared with laughter as I hit the sand,
As I woke up with sand on my ears and face,
I decided I'll never fall asleep at the beach, just in case.

Alexander Macleod (11)
Flora Stevenson Primary School, Edinburgh

Disney Cruise

D id you know there is a ghost in every room?
I can see dolphins on the cruise.
S uddenly, I heard a bang. What was that? Oh no! A boat crashed into us.
N ext, everybody was panicking, people were jumping on dolphins.
E veryone was happy that they were jumping on dolphins but they were also scared.
Y oung children and adults got on the lifeboats quickly.

C ruises are still really fun, like this one but some are scary.
R ight, everybody, stop panicking, there is a boat coming in two minutes.
U rgently, we need help.
I was squeezing my dog and my friend.
S oon, zigzag, zigzag, we are nearly at Disneyland Paris.
E xcitedly, I pinch myself and I wake up in my bed.

Sophia Elaine McRae-Ellis (10)
Flora Stevenson Primary School, Edinburgh

My Dream World!

I've just entered a world as hot as the sun,
Where the plants are as tasty as hot cross buns,
I've found a winning lottery ticket on the ground,
I can't complain about it and I can't really frown,
I found a magic lamp for my family
So they can bring my cat back for me,
There's an arcade just for me
So I can go into virtual reality,
I can play Pac-Man, it's a classic
And this world is really fantastic,
I can hear angels singing in the distance,
This world is just so ballistic!
The river is flowing and the plants are growing,
My eyes are pleased with what they see,
Oh, look, there's the sea!
It's time to leave this world behind,
It's been as nice as a lullaby.

Tristan Wake (11)
Flora Stevenson Primary School, Edinburgh

The Writer's Dream

He flew on swift wings, like a bird in a hurry,
Through the sky in a flurry,
Trying not to get muddy,
Down to the writer's study,
He opened the door with a clunk
And sat down on the bottom bunk,
He grabbed his pen and paper
And wrote about a baker,
He soon grew tired
Until he heard a gun being fired,
He ran outside and soon he cried
Because his dad had died
With a gun in his hand and some blood on the sand,
It was really hard to understand,
He woke with a start
And sat up like a dart,
He ate his tart and heard a cart,
Then a big fart,
"Yes!" he cried,
His dad had arrived.

Donald MacBeath (10)
Flora Stevenson Primary School, Edinburgh

The Haunted House

I saw a house in front of me
As spooky as Bloody Mary,
It had webbed windows and a broken door
And a roof which was really poor,
Which told me to come,
I went in with a fright,
But what could I do to be right?

Bang! The door shut behind me,
I really wish I hadn't come,
Now I heard loud sounds,
I saw a light beaming through,
I took a really tough step
And saw a bleeding skeleton,
I screamed and screamed until I couldn't,
I ran and ran
And looked behind,
And all I saw were skeletons and flying knives,
Oh, thank god, it was just a dream.

Pratheesa Minnal Sathish (11)
Flora Stevenson Primary School, Edinburgh

The Spooky Mansion Adventure

I woke up in a forest in the dark night,
With Shefdy and Wiktoria by my side,
I stood up and saw a big mansion
And yelled to Shefdy, "Look what I found!"
Wiktoria and Shefdy ran to me,
We tried to open the door but we needed a key,
I saw a key on the doorstep
And opened the door
And saw a crew of zombies coming out of the floor,
We ran full speed but Wiktoria got attacked,
So Shefdy started hitting the zombie back,
It fell to the ground and me and Shefdy found guns to kill those zombies,
Bang! went the gun, we killed those zombies,
Then we ran out.

Natalia Stolarz Szeremeta (10)
Flora Stevenson Primary School, Edinburgh

The Performers

The day of the concert creeps closer and closer,
I daren't scream it might end sooner,
As the plane lands, we board it
And soon enough, we will be there, performing
With so much flair.
We go on stage, it hugs me tight,
Keep on going, we've been so bright,
We sing, we dance all the night
And the crowd, they scream with all their might,
It's been so fun, it cannot end,
I wish we could do it all again,
I'm so excited for our next gig,
It'll be so fun and so big,
We'll write a song for you to sing along,
Because we're the performers.

Zoë Viale (10)
Flora Stevenson Primary School, Edinburgh

The Lovely And The Wicked!

Once upon a time, the sun was shining,
Below a hill that a girl and her dog were climbing,
Suddenly, a unicorn with a rainbow horn appeared,
Unfortunately, it flew into a hag thorn,
They ran past and realised they could fly away
Up into the big blue sky
So the girl fell asleep on a fluffy cloud,
She dreamed that a killer clown was in town,
She was walking and she fell down,
The scary clown wearing a crown made the girl frown,
So she was very scared when she went into that town,
Then her dog barked and woke her up!

Iris Dagg (10)
Flora Stevenson Primary School, Edinburgh

A Dream About A Vet

It started at the desk,
Thinking about what to do to be a vet,
People who were wearing white clothes
Started taking animals in,
So I thought I should try doing it,
So I asked the lady at the desk, "Can I do this one?"
She said yes, so where should I start?
It is kind of hard to know where to go because it's dark,
Then I realised I was in a car park,
Then I said it is too hard,
I will not come back next time,
It will not be so hard,
That's what it's like being a vet.

Cara Taylor (10)
Flora Stevenson Primary School, Edinburgh

The Dancing Cat

D ancing there is a cat in the mist,
A dance he is performing, down in the London streets,
N ow, I chase, he runs away on top of London Bridge,
C an't catch him, he'll run away, so why can't we talk to wash this anger away?
I like him now, he likes me back, let's hope I can keep this be,
N ext time I meet him, I hope we can eat a meal to remember for me and him,
G ot to go now, I will come back, so there the cat goes and never comes back.

William Turner (11)
Flora Stevenson Primary School, Edinburgh

The Green Land

I woke up in a green land
With a load of sand on my face,
But the cat woke up with grace,
William was already awake
And he smelt like cake, fresh out of bake,
The cat jumped onto my hand
And licked me,
I got up and looked at the free land,
I looked around and found a rope,
I heard a call and jumped to see a waterfall,
A pair of scissors lay on some hay.
I picked them up and cut the rope with a final grope,
Turns out it was just a dream
And I woke with a gleam.

James Behan (11)
Flora Stevenson Primary School, Edinburgh

My Dream Starts

Once, I had a dream,
The most amazing dream,
First, it started in my bed, just normal,
Then my mum was jumping like a kangaroo,
I was confused, like a kangaroo who can't jump,
My mum shouted in a high pitch,
"You got in!"
My mouth was open,
I could not shut it,
I was doing everything so fast,
Like an Olympian,
I got ready, went in the car,
My stomach had butterflies,
Went in but I was as slow as a turtle,
So I danced like a superstar.

Ayusma Kunwar (10)
Flora Stevenson Primary School, Edinburgh

I Once Had A Dream! A Wonderful Dream!

I once had a dream, a wonderful dream,
It all started with me,
I flew to America on a jet,
I worked as a movie star
And I was in a band,
BLSZ was our name
And money was our game,
We won as much money as we could gain,
Two hundred thousand pounds each second
And we couldn't get blamed,
I bought a mansion next to Stella, Lola and Zoe,
As well, Lauryn was my BFF and Emily as well,
And Chloe was just my friend.

Bea Murray (10)
Flora Stevenson Primary School, Edinburgh

Ghost

I enter a world of cloud and mist,
All I can see is smoke,
Then I walk over to a park,
Nothing there other than a figure in the distance,
I walk up to see who it could be,
They turn around and start chasing me,
I run as fast as Usain Bolt,
It is right behind me,
I try to hide but it can still see me,
I am considering life choices,
But then it disappears into thin air,
I start waking up, it's just a dream.

Max Cleland (10)
Flora Stevenson Primary School, Edinburgh

My Great Holiday

On my holiday, we had a great time,
Skiing and jumping in a world of mine,
Racing and running as we glided along,
In fact, we were also singing a song,
As we got home, we rested by the fire,
Watching it flicker was my desire,
We talked for hours
And then we all had showers,
We tried not to rest our head,
But then I woke up instead.

Stella Smith (10)
Flora Stevenson Primary School, Edinburgh

The Dream

D reading what might lurk in the dark, but I'll just be silent like a fart,
R unning through the moon, watching Michael Jackson do the moonwalk,
E ating roast chicken and dancing with Chewie,
A in't going back to reality,
M um tries to wake me up, so I fall asleep in my dreams.

Cameron Boyd (11)
Flora Stevenson Primary School, Edinburgh

The Bus That Can Go Anywhere

I was lost in a forest when I went outside to play,
I thought the forest was normal but I guess I was wrong,
I saw a bus that was sparkling, brand new,
I went in it since there was no bus driver telling me what to do,
When I went in, I saw a sign saying,
Shout where you want to go and may your wish come true!
I thought about it for a second,
I thought, *no way this is true!*
So I shouted, "Prove it to me then, take me to the moon!"
The engine started, then *whoosh!*
It flew into the air,
Then it landed on the moon, faster than ever,
I looked out my window
And what did I see?
I saw the moon floor,
Then I said, "Okay, I guess you proved me wrong,
Now can you take me home please, I am tired of all this fun!"

Katie Loudon (9)
Golfhill Primary School, Airdrie

Fairy Land

I went to sleep and woke up in Fairy Land,
Little fairies flying about in the sky saying hi,
I saw little fairy houses and I thought to myself,
I can't believe I'm in Fairy Land!
A fairy came flying down to me,
I was a bit scared but I felt like she was as nice as a tiny mouse,
I started to feel excited that a real fairy was in front of me,
I said hello and she said hello back and said, "My name is Fally the fairy!"
I thought that name was nice,
She took me to her house
And all I could see were couches made out of pom-poms,
As white as can be
And small little clouds as beds,
The fairy gave me a potion and I drank it,
I woke up and I figured out I was in a Fairy Land dream!

Mirryn McCormick (9)
Golfhill Primary School, Airdrie

The Magical City

The unicorn was in the magical city, wondering what was there,
Her name? She was called Ayla,
She was watching the sparkling clouds
Slowly moving through the sky,
Waiting for Lila, her fairy friend,
Lila's wings fluttered with sparkle,
Ayla saw Lila from miles,
She saw her wings sparkle with joy,
Lila finally got to the magical city,
Asking why they were here,
Ayla said, "We are magical, that's why!"
They walked to a house that was sparkling with happiness,
Lila walked upstairs, Ayla came behind her,
Lila saw something white and blue,
They walked through it,
It was sparkling clouds,
As they walked through, they saw sparkles
And they never wanted to leave,
They were never seen again!

Eilidh Mcginness (9)
Golfhill Primary School, Airdrie

Time-Travelling Nightmare

There was a portal that looked like it would take you somewhere unusual,
When you walked through the portal, everything looked immortal,
There was a magical house with a screaming green door,
Edible strawberry walls
And the most incredible room ever,
I looked with my two eyes and saw something that looked like it was about to die,
Me, my sister and my fish stepped into a world we would never forget,
You could see fifty times the planets there were before,
The planets danced with glee but then they saw my sister and me,
Everyone flew at us with trembling anger,
We ran back to the portal where it was nicer weather,
I woke up in my bed,
Me and my sister were together,
It was all just a nightmare because of the bad weather.

Ellie Easton (10)
Golfhill Primary School, Airdrie

The Revenge Of The Goalkeeper Gloves

"Bye, stinky yellow gloves,
I have a new pair of gloves and they're better!"
"I will have my revenge, goalie, mark my words,
Come out of the bin my brothers,
We must find more kits across town,"
"How about the landfill?"
"No, it is too soon,
At midnight tonight,
For now, we search bins!"
"Okay, we have got every kit in town,
Now, charge!"
Thump! Thump! Thump!
Bang!
"Revenge!"
"Look, we wanted to keep all of you,
But we couldn't because you were too smelly!"
"We won't leave without a fight!"
"Wash them!"
"What? Aarrgh!"
"Now we can keep you!"

Caleb Hamill (9)
Golfhill Primary School, Airdrie

Magical Land

Once upon a time, I was walking with a unicorn man,
He was taller than a gate that's seven-foot tall,
We were on a trip to see the very magical Ryan,
His tower was taller than a skyscraper,
We teleported up to Ryan,
He was very tall, he was eight foot like unicorn man,
While I'm only seven-point six-foot,
I said, "Can you turn us into babies at eight foot?"
"Yes, but you will go to Planet 161, okay?"
We said okay and he said, "Vouuqusududoqunqua!"
Bam! We were on Planet 161,
It was quiet, like the quietest place,
We went on flying things,
We saw our planet but it was the size of a mushroom,
We flew over and found Ryan
And lived happily ever after.

John Moultrie (9)
Golfhill Primary School, Airdrie

Trapped Away

I was taken into a room with two guards either side of me,
I had done nothing wrong,
They threw me into a room and put handcuffs on me,
As one of the guards walked out, they dropped a key,
I sat down, keeping my eye on the key until they left,
They slammed the door,
Bang!
The door went,
I ran to the key,
I tried to unlock the door but it didn't work,
I tried my handcuffs and...
It worked!
I found a loose brick,
I pulled it out and I could squeeze out,
I ran so fast,
Right past the guards and out,
They started to chase me,
I climbed up the ladder as fast as I could,
I looked back and saw them chasing me but I got away,
I was free at last!

Isla Kerr (10)
Golfhill Primary School, Airdrie

Candy Land

There was a Candy Land,
The house was as cool as a gold book,
It had a roof made out of candyfloss,
A mint choc chip cookie door
And a Smarties chocolate ice cream car,
When I walked into the kitchen, I heard a noise,
It was a slurping like someone was drinking,
It was a chocolate milkshake with chocolate bits,
The house had Oreos as the walls,
So I thought I could eat one so I wouldn't starve,
I was happy that I got candy,
But the door handle, I never knew about,
Well, nobody knew about,
I went to the Science Centre to find out,
They didn't know either,
I called it the creamy quack,
So people wouldn't get mixed up.

Aaron Alexander Fraser (9)
Golfhill Primary School, Airdrie

My Little Monster

My little monster, hiding under the bed,
My little monster makes a big noise,
My little monster comes out from under the bed,
My little monster has blue hair and a small body,
My little monster has a purple fuzzy beard,
My little monster has green spikes on his back,
My little monster said, "Hello, do you want to be my friend?"
My little monster gave me a hug,
But my little monster's green spikes pricked me!
I said, "Ow!"
My little monster felt bad for pricking me,
My little monster went back under the bed,
My little monster, please don't go!
My little monster wasn't under the bed anymore...

Erin McLaughlin (9)
Golfhill Primary School, Airdrie

The Land Of Monsters

In a land of monsters,
There was me, Cole and Lewis,
Trying to escape the land,
Feeling very weird,
Just trying to leave,
But it just couldn't go to plan,
So, we just kept trying to find new ways out,
All the greatness happens
When all the monsters fall asleep,
Just not right now,
We will escape,
We will escape when we find an exit,
It will be great!
It finally happened,
We found the exit,
We flew out on the dragon,
So grateful we had it,
We landed and said goodbye
To the dragon so sweet,
The wonderful dragon
To never be seen again.

Jack Graham Cunningham (10)
Golfhill Primary School, Airdrie

The Magical Land

Magical, magical as a magician,
I was so surprised,
I had to keep on wishing,
I was in Magical Land,
The most fun place in the galaxy,
I saw lots and lots of stuff,
But I mainly loved the fairies,
They always sang a song,
It sounded like,
"Fairies, fairies, we are the fairies,
We love, we love to paint and draw all day!
The fairies, the fairies, we tidy everything!"
I also saw unicorns, they went, "Neigh!"
And flew about the place,
I was so happy with it,
You could even say overjoyed,
I had so many adventures until...
I woke up.

Sophie Hughes (10)
Golfhill Primary School, Airdrie

Superheroes

S ometimes, I wonder if I could be a superhero,
U p above I could fly in the air,
P eeking like the sky peeks at us,
E erie, but then it happened, I became a superhero!
R eady, like the last time, then I started to whoosh in the sky like a rocket,
H igh in the sky, it felt weird,
E yed the ground like a hawk,
R eal as anything, I'm sure of it,
O n top of the buildings, flying,
E eek!
S o, then, I realised it was all a dream.

Hassan Ayub (9)
Golfhill Primary School, Airdrie

Majestic Sweet Land

One day, I was walking through a house,
It was dark and creepy,
I went into the hall, the floor was very creaky
And I fell through the floor,
I fell into a majestic sweet land,
I saw a gingerbread house,
I knocked on the toffee door
And the gingerbread man answered,
I said, "Where am I?"
"You are in Sweet Land!"
I said, "Can I come into your house?"
The couch was made of chocolate
And the stairs were ginger,
I was a bit hungry, so I ate it.

Lewis Vance (9)
Golfhill Primary School, Airdrie

The Sparkling City

The royal fairies,
One is called Tiana,
The other one is called Mia,
Mia left, she went to Candy Land,
So Tiana went on a big adventure through the Sparkling City,
She met a unicorn she had never seen before,
She was called Rechel, she had a sparkling horn,
She said, "Are you the royal fairy, Tiana?"
"Yes!"
"Come with me and we can have some tea!"
So they had some tea and went off into the candyfloss clouds.

Keira Brown (10)
Golfhill Primary School, Airdrie

The Haunted Dream

Once upon a dream, I came across a castle,
It had enormous big black walls
With lots of enormous red scratches.
It had wooden stairs and lots of big cracks.
Me and my dog, Scamper, carried on.
An old lady came out
And me and my dog went in.
The door closed.
The old lady came back and saw us.
I saw a book that said Miss Trunchpoll,
I opened it and she got sucked in the book.
I locked it and ran home with Scamper.

Rory Anderson (9)
Golfhill Primary School, Airdrie

The Stars

T he stars shine bright like the sun in the noon,
H undreds of them and they all disappear soon,
E legant in the night but gone in the day.

S tars are beautiful, I wish they could stay,
T heir shining light shows the way,
A fter all, they're balls of flame,
R ed and bright, some say they're lame,
S tay all night but to see again, wait all day!

Lauren Robertson (10)
Golfhill Primary School, Airdrie

Candy Land

I was walking to school with friends,
When we saw a magical portal,
We stepped through the purple and black,
It felt like we were being attacked,
We saw a house surrounded by candyfloss and trees,
A car made out of ice cream, this was my favourite dream,
There was a roof made out of fudge,
I gave my friend a nudge,
The walls were made out of Oreo,
It certainly didn't taste horrible!

Jack Grant (9)
Golfhill Primary School, Airdrie

The Fight

T here were two castles about to fight,
H elpful, but not to each other,
E ven I saw it, it gave me quite a fright,

F ive minutes later, the dragons got released,
I had never seen a zombie before,
G ive me a second, I thought they were herbivores!
H i there, I think a zombie ate me,
T oo late, I should have hidden behind a tree.

Lewis Anderson (9)
Golfhill Primary School, Airdrie

Candy Town

In Candy Town, you can do what you want,
Everyone was very happy!
Until an elephant with big tusks
Came to destroy the gingerbread family's house,
Stomp!
Me, Gingerbread Jessy and Candy Cane Junior
Went to fight him,
We tried to kill him,
But we only scared him
And told him never to come back.

Noah Magennis (9)
Golfhill Primary School, Airdrie

The Bed Monster

I go into my room and see,
The bed monster as big as can be,
Her eyes as blue as the sky,
Her mouth as red as an apple,
Her fur as pink as candyfloss,
Her friends so evil,
Her eyes as red as a chilli
Her mouth as pink as a lollipop,
Her fur is red as well,
The bed monster is now my friend.

Lucy Marshall (10)
Golfhill Primary School, Airdrie

Crystal Custard Creams

I was eating custard creams
And then I went into my dream,
I looked behind me
To see a man who was emerald-green,
His name was Crystal Chris
And behind his back was a shopping list,
On it were crystal custard creams,
Then I realised this was the best dream!

Caleb Young (10)
Golfhill Primary School, Airdrie

Transylvania

The town as eerie as a cave,
Roads filled up with stones
And there, I saw a vampire
And decided to build a campfire,
He had pale skin and crooked hands,
He could fly across all the land,
I felt so scared, I had the fear,
He flew away and left me here.

Cole Ferguson (9)
Golfhill Primary School, Airdrie

Dance And Dream

D ancer, Bella, good as a ballerina
A nd better at dancing when she has a dream,
N ext time I saw her, I got so inspired,
C hloe and I ended up better than her,
E ven better than a dream.

Ava Keenan (9)
Golfhill Primary School, Airdrie

Dreams

T here was a group of children who ventured into a haunted house,
E agerly, Gerry, a small, red-haired boy disappeared into a room, he loved exploring,
"R un!" he screamed, returning to the group, whilst being chased by a scary skeleton,
R attling a large broom, the skeleton chased the children along the dark corridor, into a large kitchen full of cobwebs,
I ona, Gerry's friend, shouted, "It's a dead end, the only way out is by the window!"
F iercely, Thomas picked up a pot and pan and ran towards the skeleton, "Quick, everyone, climb out the window!"
Y ellow bats came flying into the window, stopping the children from escaping, the skeleton started laughing, shouting, "There is no escape, children!"
I n a split second, Gerry covered the skeleton's face with a pot so it couldn't see, it tripped and fell down the laundry,
"N ow, everyone, run for your life!" cried Iona, they all ran out of the house, through the forest and back home,
G erry woke up in bed with his heart beating very fast, "Wow, was that a dream?" he asked himself.

John Keenan (10)
Heriot Primary School, Paisley

Lollipop Town

One stormy night, I snuggled in my bed,
Eagerly waiting for what dream lay ahead,
My head hit my pillow that smelt like a candy cane,
I fell asleep and hopped on my imaginary train,
"Where will my mind take me today?
How about Lollipop Town?"
Hey presto, I flew up, up and away!
I finally landed and I couldn't believe my eyes,
I looked up and there were pink candyfloss clouds in the sky,
I saw fairies and all sorts of wonderful treats,
But ten feet away was a forest full of sweets!
I sprinted to the forest, I saw a weird shadow,
I heard a weird noise, I thought it was a horse,
But it was a unicorn!
I spotted it from miles away,
All I wanted to do was go up to it and play,
"Argh!" Suddenly, I woke up and screamed,
But then I remembered it was just a dream,
I started feeling sad because I couldn't finish my adventure,
But I will have another one, maybe with the same beautiful creature.

Ellie Louise McLaren (10)
Heriot Primary School, Paisley

Night Terrors

Midnight arrives on this cloudy night,
Dreams leave and nightmares arise
And the thunderstorm comes with a lot of might,
I finally drift off, awaiting sunrise.

An alien landscape is the first thing I see,
A dark, creepy mansion is right behind me,
I gaze in terror at what lies ahead,
It's a ten-foot spider on the mansion roof.

I can't move a muscle, I'm as cold as rock,
It spots me and jumps, it's in front of me now,
I prepare for the end as the spider lunges,
I sit up with a look of terror, take a deep breath, I'm awake.

James Hunter (10)
Heriot Primary School, Paisley

The Magic Elephant

M y heart skips a beat,
A s, to my surprise,
G reeting me so nicely,
I s an elephant with cute eyes,
"**C** ome here!" she said, as she flew in the sky,

"**E** lephant, give me some powers,
L et me be like you, I may fly!
E lephant, can you?"
"**P** ractice starts tomorrow,
H ow high can you fly?
A tmosphere perhaps? I'd better go, bye!"
"**N** ight night!"
T o my surprise, I find myself back in bed with no elephant powers.

Alex Reekie (10)
Heriot Primary School, Paisley

The Magical Dream

I was going to bed and I went to sleep,
Suddenly, I was teleported to this big city,
I could fly!
Oh, I wish it was all real.
I had a wand, so maybe that's why I could fly,
I could also do magic things,
I was all by myself and I felt really sad,
I wanted a friend who could fly,
I felt so excited, amazed and supreme,
I was on top of the world,
I was just so impressed,
But all good things have an ending,
I ran out of magic,
I woke up
Which transported me back,
It was all just a dream, now I'm in my bed.

Riley Meechan (11)
Heriot Primary School, Paisley

Big Game Dreams

F ans screaming from the stadium,
O pposition warming up,
O ut of the tunnel we come, butterflies in my belly,
T ime for kick-off, I look round to the cameras, can't believe I'm on telly,
B ack to Ryan as I pass the ball, his touch is second to none,
A huge roar fills the stadium as I smash it past their number one,
L eft it all on the pitch, coaches couldn't be happier with all thirteen,
L astly came the time I hate, time to wake up, what a night it's been!

Jamie James McKechnie (11)
Heriot Primary School, Paisley

The Blizzard

As I waddle through the stormy blizzard,
I see something that looks like a wizard,
As I draw closer, I can see a big, huge thing
Staring at me,
My hand shakes as I go to touch it,
My hands gain warmth like a man getting fit,
As the blizzard calms down, I know I'm not going to drown,
There was a penguin in sight,
I knew I could really use a penguin at night,
I wake up in the morning,
I can hear my mum calling,
I realise it's all a dream!

Morgan Gallacher (11)
Heriot Primary School, Paisley

The Lost Dinosaur

Logan and I went to Barshaw Park,
Suddenly, it went really dark!
We turned around and saw
A ten-foot dinosaur!
We screamed and shouted, "Help!"
But nobody was around to hear us yelp,
He had crumbled everything in his way,
Was this a dream or was it real today?
We were shocked and scared and ran for our life,
Let's hope we could escape the strife,
The dino caught up with us and as we turned around...
Gulp!

Rory Young (10)
Heriot Primary School, Paisley

Originality

O riginal means you're unique in every way,
R esourceful in your actions,
I ndependently strong every day,
G uardian of your thoughts,
I nspire people all day,
N ever doubt yourself,
A lways believe in yourself,
L ive for tomorrow,
I have lots to share,
T omorrow, a new adventure,
Y ou are original.

Keira Abbie (10)
Heriot Primary School, Paisley

Superheroes

S uperpowers make you stronger,
U nder the shade of fights,
P ower up with the heroes,
E nergy is within us,
R espect the heroes of life,
H elp the good,
E vacuate if needed,
R unning as fast as Captain America,
O bviously, Thor is the best,
E xcited, or not, run and fight,
S et in the park.

Kenzie Milne (10)
Heriot Primary School, Paisley

Monsters!

M onsters haunt my dreams every night,
"**O** h no!" I scream as I get such a fright,
N ot only are they big and scary,
S ome are even pink and hairy,
T hey always come out, night and day,
E lla hurt my foot so I may need an X-ray,
R ound and round the room they go,
S inging songs that I don't know.

Hannah McCallum (10)
Heriot Primary School, Paisley

Famous Dancer

The music begins and what can I see?
Hundreds of people staring at me,
I'm on the stage with KW,
We start to dance,
Everyone goes quiet,
The music ends and what do I see?
Hundreds of people cheering for me!
My mum is so proud,
She's shouting so loud,
I feel like a superstar,
I hope I go far.

Sophie Karen Help (11)
Heriot Primary School, Paisley

My Garden

I have a beautiful garden
Where I can play and dig,
I run and have fun,
I love sunflowers looking at the sun,
Roses pose like a wonderful lady,
Daffodils look like stars in my garden,
Robins are looking for food,
Squirrels are playing around the garden,
I love my garden so much.

Marcus Issac (10)
Heriot Primary School, Paisley

My Best Friend

H amish is my handsome dog,
A ll my friends love Hamish,
M y nickname for him is Oreo,
I love Hamish.
S chool would be even better if I could take Hamish with me,
H amish is my best friend.

Amber McKinnon (10)
Heriot Primary School, Paisley

Dreaming

D reams are magical all the time and never end,
R abbits hopping in the fields and back to their houses in your dreams,
E very dream is good and fantastic but some are bad and horrifying,
A mazing dreams will always be beside you and in your memories,
M onkeys eating bananas in the jungle, swinging from tree to tree in your quiet dreams,
I magine you are in Gran Canaria with your granny and grandpa,
N ightmares are sometimes in your dreams but they fight away the night,
G oing on holidays in Gran Canaria underneath the palms.

Liliana Biros (7)
Hillside School, Portlethen

Dreams

D elicious, lovely ice lollies in the hot sun are lovely melting in my mouth,
R eading precious stories and eating golden toffees,
E merging from the lovely light on a summer's day,
A mazing friends I visit all the time in my wonderful, tall castle,
M iming lots of cool shows are fun in my dreams,
I love Scarlett, Keira and Grace telling me all their secrets in my dreams,
N athanael swims underwater to save me in my dreams,
G ran is the best in the world and gives me everything I want in my dreams.

Emma Miller (7)
Hillside School, Portlethen

Dream Poem

D aring, dancing dreams fill my tiny brain,
R eciting the same dream over and over again,
E vening has come and now it's time to have new, different dreams,
A silly, sunny, sweet dream will make you laugh so much,
M aybe, one magical day, my dream may come true as well as yours,
I ncredible interpretations of your dancing dreams,
N ightmares make you scream in horror,
G iggling girls and boys dancing to their totally crazy dreams.

Inioluwa Adejugba (7)
Hillside School, Portlethen

Dream Poem

D azzling dreams about cute rainbow unicorns that are sparkly,
R ainbows sparkling for you, gleaming in your dreams,
E xciting dreams always are the best dreams,
A mazing dreams can be magnificent to sleep more to carry on the story,
M agical Marvel dreams can be adventures,
I n your head, you are dreaming, it is not actually happening,
N ightmares are scary and they make you scream,
G oing to bed can be fun to dream.

Megan Lucy Kenyon (7)
Hillside School, Portlethen

Dreaming

D ark nights, nice dreams in your cosy bed at home,
R ainbow cookies and doughnuts in lovely dreams, bad dreams are bad to have,
E ven when you have a nightmare think about something else,
A wesome candyfloss and sweets to eat in a wonderful dream,
M indful words said in your dreams,
I ncredible dreams are good to imagine,
N asty dreams stick in your head all the time,
G ood dreams I like to have.

Hannah Milne (7)
Hillside School, Portlethen

Dreams

D ream toys only come true on Christmas Eve,
R eimagine something in your life and make it better,
E ven Santa has nightmares, everyone does,
A mazing dreams, amazing life,
M agical unicorns and diamonds, dragons and giants,
I magine something and make it come true,
N ight lights on, eyes closed, night night,
G iants live up in the rainbow clouds.

Shyloh Duncan (8)
Hillside School, Portlethen

Dreaming

D ark, scary dreams can be scary sometimes,
R obins chirping in my dreams that are so cute,
E veryone has different dreams that can be happy or sad,
A wesome dreams can be lots of fun,
M agical rainbows appear in my dreams,
I ncredible thoughts make incredible dreams,
N ever-ending dreams keep me awake,
G oing to bed is fun when I read books.

Olivia Abbey Davie (8)
Hillside School, Portlethen

Dreams

D reams are awesome when you dream about winning, a lot of fun when you go away,
R acing cars are amazing but my dream is to get remote-controlled racing cars,
E llie Elephant when he falls asleep, he dreams about waving his big feet,
A dventure dreams are my favourite because I love dinosaurs that I see,
M emory dreams are my greatest because I remember them in a way.

Lewis Tawse (7)
Hillside School, Portlethen

Dreams

D isgraceful dreams are dark and terrifying,
R ainbows are beautiful in Dreamland, the way they light up the sky,
E legant dreams are the best because they do not terrify you!
A dventures are the type of dream I would like to dream,
M ythical animals come to me in my dreams like unicorns,
S tories help me to go to incredible dreams, my happy place.

Keira Jackson (7)
Hillside School, Portlethen

Dreams

D reams can be horrifying and sometimes magical,
R emember your good dreams and forget your bad,
E very dream could be magical or haunted,
A nightmare can be very scary and horrifying,
M y dreams are to explore the ocean and swim with salmon, card fish, dolphins and sharks,
S ome of my dreams are about the Taj Mahal.

Ashrith Padakanti (7)
Hillside School, Portlethen

Dreaming

D reams can always come true,
R eading a book before I go to bed,
E very dream has a happy ending,
A dventures happen in my dreams,
M y dream was about unicorns,
I always have glorious dreams,
N o awful dreams come while good dreams are happening,
G ood people always have fantastic dreams.

Elvita Srivastava (7)
Hillside School, Portlethen

Dreams

D ark dreams going away, away,
R ainbow sweets are fading away,
E very dream you imagine, it is true,
A mazing imaginative things are not real,
M agical I am in dreams,
I ncredible things are working, they make
N aughty dreams, very bad, you wake up from
G reat, amazing adventurous dreams.

Harriet Conner (7)
Hillside School, Portlethen

Dreams

D ark, peaceful dreams,
R ainbows glistening in the scorching air,
E ven though bad dreams are scary, I still love dreams,
A mazing unicorns are bright blue and pink, they love to watch Marvel movies,
M indful dreams going in my wonderful brain,
S unny, bright people love to walk down the unexpected corridor.

Indy Hunter (7)
Hillside School, Portlethen

Dreams

D reamy dreams are special and gleaming but dreadful dreams are creepy,
R hyming words are part of your dreams but always stand together,
E dible slime is scrumptious and lovely but always awesome,
A mazing dreams can come true but it can be very adventurous,
M agical dreams are the best of all dreams and are fabulous.

Amy Mitchell (8)
Hillside School, Portlethen

Dreaming

D reams are magical and fun,
R eading a nice book before bed helps me sleep,
E very dream can come true,
A beautiful dream will make you happy,
M agnificent dreams are amazing,
I love dreaming because I always have good ones,
N ightmares are super scary,
G reat dreams make me happy.

Emmie Milne (8)
Hillside School, Portlethen

Dreams

D ragons in your dreams breathing burning hot fire,
R eading before I go to bed helps me sleep,
E ating yummy sweets in each Dreamland,
A pple toffees and lollipops getting stickier in each land as I go on,
M agical places with mythical animals in them, wow!
S pending all my money on electronics and DVDs.

Mason McRobb (8)
Hillside School, Portlethen

Dream

D reams about driving Lamborghinis and surfing zombies are awesome,
R ainbows in your dreams when it's raining are mysterious, like an elephant with one ear,
E pic dreams are fantastic, like getting sucked into a game,
A mazing dreams, like having ice cream, are the best,
M agical dragons trying to eat you up.

Cameron Tempest (7)
Hillside School, Portlethen

Dreams

D reams are sometimes magical or horrifying,
R emember your sweet dreams in the fluffy clouds,
E very dream has a happy ending,
A mazing dreams are always beside you and the bad ones are gone,
M y magical worlds come to life, swimming in the oceans,
S ometimes you can believe in your dreams.

Aston Pender (8)
Hillside School, Portlethen

Dreaming

D reams are amazing and they come to life,
R eading makes you dream,
E very dream opens the door to a new world,
A mazing dreams come true,
M oney and Lamborghinis are the best dreams,
I never have nightmares,
N ew worlds unfolding,
G reat dreams throw out bad dreams.

Chimzara Victor Roberts (7)
Hillside School, Portlethen

Dreams

D reams are perfect and sometimes bad, remember the good dreams,
R emember the good dreams and don't remember the bad dreams,
E very dream is different,
A dventure dreams are so good,
M y dreams are so crazy that they came true,
S o many dreams to look forward to.

Jamie Moncur (8)
Hillside School, Portlethen

Dreams

D ark dreams we have, always, but just think about unicorns and rainbows,
R iding on pink, fluffy unicorns in my mind,
E very night I have exciting dreams,
A mazing stories help me get off to sleep,
M ice crawling in my dreams,
S uper dreams we always have at bedtime.

Emma Lewis (7)
Hillside School, Portlethen

Dreams

D reams can come true if you believe in them,
R emembering your sweet dreams so you are happy and magical,
E xpectations are great in your dreams,
A wakening things make me smile,
M agical dreams will always come true,
S ecret dreams are fun to watch in your sleep.

Ella Milne (7)
Hillside School, Portlethen

Dream Poetry

D reams are good for you when you're sleeping,
R emembering your sweet dreams so you are happy and magical,
E veryone has good dreams and bad dreams, which are not good,
A mazing dreams come true,
M agical dreams while I sleep,
S weet dreams come true.

Olivia Milne (8)
Hillside School, Portlethen

Dreams

D ream about all the things you can think of,
R eading bedtime stories makes me go to sleep,
E xpecting your dreams to come true,
A mazing things make me smile when I sleep,
M y magical world comes to life,
S ome dreams wake me and make me smile.

Abbie Pirie (7)
Hillside School, Portlethen

Dream Poem

D reaming all about Rubix cubes,
R emarkable rainbows are extraordinary,
E xciting memories for everybody in the universe,
A mazing people are everywhere I go, it's so crazy,
M indful meditation, the most marvellous in the whole world.

Harry Auld (8)
Hillside School, Portlethen

Dreams

D reams are fun because they make me happy,
R emember your happy dreams and don't forget,
E veryone has different, fun dreams,
A mazing dreams always come true,
M ystery dreams are always fun,
S pecial dreams are very fun.

Ryan Weng (8)
Hillside School, Portlethen

Dreams

D reams are filled with happiness,
R emember that there are good and bad dreams,
E xpectations are great in your dreams,
A mazing dreams are full of fun,
M agnificent fairies dancing around,
S pecial worlds I have discovered.

Jessica Ellie Robertson (8)
Hillside School, Portlethen

Dreams Poem

D reamy, beautiful, fun dreams, they are really incredible,
R ainbow dreams bouncing in your head,
E legant dreams are fun and cool,
A t night, all my amazing adventures come to life,
M ysterious, mythical dreams never come true to me.

Komeno Jaden Obaruakporo (7)
Hillside School, Portlethen

Dreams

D reams are nothing but magical,
R eading makes you dream,
E very dream is magical or horrifying,
A beautiful dream will make you happy,
M y magnificent dreams are about unicorns and rainbows,
S ome dreams are terrifying.

Ruby Walker (7)
Hillside School, Portlethen

Dreams

D reams dance through your head,
R emember your good dreams and forget your bad dreams,
E verybody has horrid dreams,
A n amazing adventure to enjoy,
M y favourite dream would be about hamsters,
S leep time for everyone.

Daniel Robert Murray (8)
Hillside School, Portlethen

Dreams

D reams may come true,
R emember the good dreams that have passed,
E very good dream has a good experience,
A lot of nightmares are horrifying,
M y dreams will come to life,
S ome dreams are nightmares, some are not.

Ife Adeyemi (7)
Hillside School, Portlethen

Dreams

D reams are dreams or nightmares as well,
R eading before bed,
E very one of my dreams has a Pokémon and the SS Anne,
A mazing things make you smile,
M ake your dreams come true,
S weet dreams make me sleep.

Flynn Taylor (7)
Hillside School, Portlethen

Dreams

D reams can be horrible or interesting,
R ead before you go to bed,
E very dream is fantastic and unique,
A mazing dreams come true,
M y dream is about exploring the ocean,
S ome people have good and bad dreams.

Campbell Stephen (7)
Hillside School, Portlethen

Dreams

D oves fly so softly in my dream,
R unning in amazing imagination,
E very dream has a happy ending,
A dream is just the beginning of a new world,
M um and Dad give me a kiss in my bed,
S un shining in my world.

Dara Shadare (8)
Hillside School, Portlethen

Dreams Poem

D ark at night does not scare me,
R ainbows in my dreams make me happy,
E xploring dreams is amazing,
A Lamborghini please, I thought in my dream,
M agical dreams make me happy,
S ee dreams in your mind.

Leah Kemp (7)
Hillside School, Portlethen

Dreams

D reams are mostly good but some are bad,
R eading before bed helps me sleep,
E very dream has a happy ending,
A dream is your imagination,
M y magical world comes to life,
S afely sleeping in my bed.

Lewis Michie (7)
Hillside School, Portlethen

Dreams

D reams come every night,
R emember, some dreams are bad and some are good,
E veryone has dreams,
A dream can make you talk in your sleep,
M any animals live in dreams,
S ome people have dreams.

Maddisyn McInnes (7)
Hillside School, Portlethen

Dreams

D readful dreams make you sad,
R eading Harry Potter on a pitch-black night helps me sleep,
E vening is here and it is night,
A dragon is scary in dreams,
M agical dreams end in a happy ending.

Mason John Gill (7)
Hillside School, Portlethen

Dreams

D reams are coming true,
R eading bedtime stories,
E xtremely exciting memories for me,
A dventures in my mind now,
M emories are good fun to make,
S wimming in a pool of rainbows.

Maisie Ruby Fraser (7)
Hillside School, Portlethen

Dreams

D reams can come true,
R eading makes you dream,
E veryone dreams about something,
A mazing dreams can come true,
M y dreams are about exploring the ocean,
S wimming with dolphins.

Cooper Inglis (7)
Hillside School, Portlethen

Dreams

D reams are amazing,
R iding on my pony is amazing,
E very evening I read a bedtime story,
A dragon crawled into my bed,
M agical dreams are amazing,
S uper dreams are awesome.

Nathan Laing (7)
Hillside School, Portlethen

Dream

D ream big, dream bright, dream all night,
R ainbows glistening off the nutritious water,
E ating enormous ice cream that is yummy,
A wesome places I travel to,
M ajestical unicorns.

Devin Cameron (7)
Hillside School, Portlethen

Dream Poetry

D reams are nothing but magic,
R eading at night,
E very dream comes true for me,
A wesome dreams feel amazing,
M y dreams are funny,
S afe, lovely nights.

Chloe South (8)
Hillside School, Portlethen

Nature Nightmare

I trudge,
Slowly and wearily on,
Under the endless canopy,
I shiver,
Shadows dance from unmoving plants,
The wind howls but doesn't blow,
I stumble on,
Again, I shiver,
The stuffy air full of sinister magic,
The forest silent as if all the life has been swept from the trees,
A small rustle,
I see, in the centre of the clearing,
A gigantic tiger with yellow eyes and glistening white fangs,
I turn and run back into the undergrowth,
The tiger running low behind me,
Closing the gap,
I look back, just as the tiger springs,
I feel pain and blood, then darkness,
I wake, drenched in cold sweat,
I shiver.

Felix Musgrave-Dance (9)
Kilchattan Primary School, Kilchattan

Mister Sorrow

Mister Sorrow is trying to scare us,
"Dribbling and drooling and..."
His long, slow murmur loses my interest.

I hear a scream,
Someone in pain,
I yell to my classmates,
A thundering clatter of feet on stairs
And the excited babble of children,
Teachers leap out of classrooms,
Flummoxed by the pandemonium,
Only to be flattened against the walls.

As the screaming grows louder,
The children speed up,
Soon, we come to the printing room,
Where we find the door is locked,
With a loud splintering of wood,
The door gives way under the strain
Of keeping back the tide
Of children, all cramming to get closer.

Inside, there is carnage,
The whole room is splattered
With scarlet splodges,

In the midst of a pile of dead students,
A bony hand reaches out to me,
I turn to run, but a steel-iron grip,
Grabs me by the shoulder and spins me around,
I smell his foul breath,
I see his red fangs as sharp as daggers,
Closing in on my neck...

"Alice... *Alice... Alice!...*"
Mister Sorrow stands in front of me,
The whole class is staring,
Is that a gleam of evil I see?

Rosie Musgrave-Dance (10)
Kilchattan Primary School, Kilchattan

You're Not Awake

I dreamed a dream,
So big and wild,
I could run so fast and touch the sky,
With multicoloured meadows and blossoming trees,
The songs of the birds and the hum of the bees,
Then, at my feet, there was a snake,
It was long and scaly and had bold, black eyes
And to my surprise, it spoke four words,
"You are not awake!"
It slithered away and left me there,
Alone in the world, the darkness falling,
A chill in the air, I was scared,
I closed my eyes and screwed them tight
And when they are opened,
I was warm in my bed.

Eve Liddell (9)
Kilchattan Primary School, Kilchattan

In The Sky

Haiku poetry

Once upon a dream,
I was flying through the sky,
Bright blue like a stream.

Some swans passed by me,
White and shimmering like gold,
Happy as can be.

A waterfall flowed,
All glittering and shining,
I stared when it glowed.

Trees below happy,
Luscious green, dazzling brightly
And looking sappy.

Suddenly, I whirred,
I was waking from dreaming
And I slowly stirred.

Eleanor Grieve (9)
Kilchattan Primary School, Kilchattan

The Monster Under The Bed

In the middle of the night,
I got a big fright,
I felt a bump on my mattress,
Like I'd been pricked by a cactus.

From under the bed
Came a creature with horns on his head,
I got a feeling inside my heart
Like it had been hit by a dart.

I thought a spider was running up my back,
I was scared the monster was about to attack,
Then I started to worry,
I hugged a teddy that was furry.

I saw the monster's spiky tail,
Then it started to rain and hail,
Next, came thunder
And I started to wonder
What was going on in my little room
Before I heard a big boom.

For, the monster had collapsed to the floor
And said, "Ouch, that was sore!"
After, he went red
And clambered back under the bed.

In the morning, I worried that
The monster was still there
But when I felt the bump was gone
I knew it was a dream all along.

Jessica Mitchell (8)
Knowetop Primary School, Motherwell

The Pug On The Rug

I was in my bed,
My head was red,
I had a dream
I'd never seen,
I walked into a hall,
I saw mouldy walls,
I looked in front, it was a rug,
On it was a cute little pug,
I went to clap,
It was having a nap,
I left it alone,
It was eating a bone,
I heard a sound,
I jumped off the ground,
I went upstairs,
I saw three bears,
I jumped on a chair,
I was so scared,
There was blood dripping,
I was kicking,
A person stood, holding a knife,
I screamed with fright,
He looked at me,
I looked at him,

I ran downstairs,
Past the bears,
I bit my tongue,
I travelled to when I was young,
I felt free
With glee,
I saw a pug,
It looked like the one on the rug,
There was blood dripping from the ceiling,
My skin was peeling,
Argh!
I sat up quickly,
It was just a dream
I'd never seen.

Isla Kennedy (8)
Knowetop Primary School, Motherwell

The Clown In My Room

I was lying in my bed,
Then I felt a little poke on the back of my head,
I turned around and got a scare
To see a clown standing there,
He chased me around my room for ages,
Then he took off a chain that you would use for cages,
He tied me to it and pulled me close,
Then he began to boast,
"I am in charge here, do what I say,
Nothing can get in my way!"
Thud! I turned around,
The clown slipped on some mud,
I was relieved to see the clown knocked out,
Though, I still had to try not to shout,
It started to get late,
Then I realised he was going to use me as bait,
Then I jumped into bed
And put a pillow at the back of my head,
Then I woke up and told my brother
I had a nightmare,
But he didn't seem to care!

Francesca Muir (8)
Knowetop Primary School, Motherwell

The Vibrant Unicorn And Cat Show

Once, I had a dream,
It was like a galaxy galore!
I heard a really loud bang,
So I went outside to see where
It was coming from.
It was the same sound,
It was night,
That's the time I got a big fright,
There it was again,
Bang! Bang! Bang!
I was getting closer and closer until,
It was a unicorn and a cat
With superpowers, they were flying,
The unicorn's fur was cold
But it was bold,
Then they put on a show,
It was like a vibrant bow!
Soon, they knew to never fight
And give me a fright!

Fizah Arshad Nawaz (9)
Knowetop Primary School, Motherwell

My Dreamland

When I was asleep,
I was cosied up in bed,
I felt dizzy,
Right inside my head.

Then I felt like I woke up,
I strode out of bed,
I made a big thump.

In front of me
Was a portal,
I stepped inside
And felt immortal.

When I stepped out,
I was in a dream,
Then I saw a big, big beam.

It was from a unicorn
With its magnificent horn,
I saw its wings
And heard its little bell ring.

It wanted me to ride it,
But I apologised and said no

Because I got out of bed,
It was time to go.

I went through the portal
And strode into bed,
Then I woke up but still rested my head.

Maisie Watters (8)
Knowetop Primary School, Motherwell

The Battle

Once, there was a town,
At the time, the weather had a frown,
There were high-level knights,
Training for a battle of their life,
A stingy old chief was giving them tips
To survive with ease,
A few hours later, they found a crater,
With a bunker to go in,
The chief said, "Go!"
But they said, "Woah!"
And they went straight in,
Then the chief unlocked the lasers
And their smiles were gone,
Mark, the best knight,
came charging in,
But he saw an injured kid.

Cameron Angus Hill (8)
Knowetop Primary School, Motherwell

The Dreamland

It's a giant purple galaxy,
With a really big capacity,
It is made up of giant islands,
The middle one is the royal land,
There are giant forests made of candy canes,
Infested with unicorns with pretty manes,
The royal palace is big and black,
With double oak doors at the front and back,
There are lakes of pure melted chocolate,
People who go there come back late,
There are lots of tame dinos
On an island full of roses.

Daniel Fiddes (8)
Knowetop Primary School, Motherwell

The Footballer's Dream

I was walking down the road
With a golden boot on my foot,
I was practising with a football
Up and down the hall,
I was holding the golden boot
And everyone was cheering,
The next day was Wednesday
And I scored the last-minute goal very fast,
In the game, I got named Top Man
And it felt really good,
I got fame,
All the other teams got shame,
This is my dream
And what a team I have!

Ross Mitchell (7)
Knowetop Primary School, Motherwell

Blacksmith

Hello there! I'm a blacksmith,
There is the fourth customer,
Now there's the fifth!
He wants his weapon,
I'd better get to work,
I'll work hard to give him his pitchfork,
First, I find the boiler,
Put in some gold,
When it's finished boiling,
I put it in the mould,
I hammer the points so it stays sharp,
I then have a break and eat a Magikarp.

Marc McGill (9)
Knowetop Primary School, Motherwell

The Spooky House

Once upon a time
It was spooky and it was light,
It was Halloween at night,
So it started long ago,
So, I went to a house
Full of fright, I had a nightmare,
The roof had blood dripping
From upstairs,
The blood was light,
Then granny ate me at night,
Then I woke up, two days later,
I was at the hospital,
I was so frightened,
My family was there!

Aaron Gribbon (7)
Knowetop Primary School, Motherwell

A Very Random Dream!

One day, I was walking down the road
And I saw an old bit of wood
And it was very mouldy
And then I went back home
And it was sunny,
So I went in my cool big pool
And then it was a school day
And then I went into class
And it was made of glass
And then I went home
And I went to get changed,
And then I blinked
And everything was pink.

Sophie Cowie (8)
Knowetop Primary School, Motherwell

On Holiday

I went in first class
And over Japan, I passed,
When I got to Florida, I saw a mouse,
In our front garden, next to the house,
After, I went into the pool
And then I saw a bull,
Next, I got a horse
And then I took it back to my house,
Nearly every night I ate
Really good meat,
The next day, I went to the theme park
And then I saw a big mark.

Harry Greve (8)
Knowetop Primary School, Motherwell

A Haunted House

I'd just moved house
And I had already seen a mouse,
Then I came across two spiders
That were as big as tigers,
When I heard there were clowns
In town,
I saw dragons
Painting wagons,
Scary people walked the halls,
But then it was two clowns,
So I moved house
Before I saw a mouse
And I ended up in another house,
I stayed in that house.

Olivia Picken (8)
Knowetop Primary School, Motherwell

Under The Sea

Under the sea
I can see
A mythical place that's waiting for me,
I saw fish,
I saw sharks,
I saw fish, they looked delish,
I loved the skeletons,
The shipwrecks
And the old, sharp shark teeth,
I saw coral,
Reefs
And clam shells too,
I loved my adventure
Under the sea.

Matthew Pettigrew (9)
Knowetop Primary School, Motherwell

I Had A Dream

I had a dream
To play for a football team.
I got a new ball
And I played in the hall.
I got to play for Tottenham Hotspur,
If I work hard I'll get to prosper.
In the Champions League,
We'll win it twice in a row,
It might be hard
But I'll give it a go!

Callum Johnstone (8)
Knowetop Primary School, Motherwell

Gotta Go Fast

Sonic is so fast,
He's always first,
He's never last,
He always defeats Eggman
Without a plan,
He has a sidekick, Tails,
Who really loves whales,
Tails also has a plane,
Sometimes, it rains,
That was my dream,
I was Sonic, what a team!

Cameron David McFarlane (7)
Knowetop Primary School, Motherwell

The Octopus

Under the sea, I could see
An octopus as small as can be,
He had three babies,
They liked jelly babies,
He had a wife,
Who was quite nice,
All of them had fun,
When they played the drum,
If his children were bad
They would definitely be sad.

Harry Jenkins (8)
Knowetop Primary School, Motherwell

My Old Classroom

I got a fright
When I saw the sight
Of some smashed glass
In my class.
I looked around
Heard a sound
And then the wall
Took a big fall
And I ran out
With a big, big shout!

Calum Preston (8)
Knowetop Primary School, Motherwell

Sky High

Everything went upside down
So I looked up with a frown,
The sky was the ground
And the land was the sky,
I thought I would fall because I was up so high!

Cameron Mills Begley (7)
Knowetop Primary School, Motherwell

Sky High

The ground turned into the sky
And my friend was up very high,
He was hot, sweaty and very sad
And he was also very mad!

Luke Craig (7)
Knowetop Primary School, Motherwell

She

she's beautiful,
she's every colour of the sunrise
and her smile's brighter than the full moon,
she's sound, sight and colour, every colour of the rainbow,
she's the fiery sunset orange and royal purple
and dark blue and créme white,
she's my everything.

I dream of us going to a special place only we know of,
I dream of travelling somewhere away from the world,
I dream of spending evenings in small, quiet cafés,
sipping tea and eating cake,
we'd then go to a peaceful park and talk about whatever,
we'd talk about books, TV, school, work, friends, old and new experiences,
we'd lie in bed, on our backs, just enjoying each other's presence,
while listening to any genre of lo-fi,
we'd awkwardly dance to the Wii theme song,
then just dance awkwardly to any playlist of songs,
we'd then go to the balcony or back garden and fall asleep underneath the beautiful night sky
while listening to a relaxing melody played by a piano on Spotify.

she is every colour of the rainbow,
she is the colour of fireworks and bright neon signs and bubble tea and blue skies and starry nights,
she is whom I longed for
and I wish I could tell her in real life.

her motto in life is 'the realest people don't have a lot of friends',
I pondered on her wise words for a while
and I realised it was as true as can be.

my motto in life is, 'your skin isn't paper, don't cut it,
your face isn't a mask, don't hide it,
your size isn't a book, don't judge it,
your heart isn't a door, don't close it,
your life isn't a movie, don't end it',
she then pondered on my words for a while
and thought it was very inspirational.

she is aesthetic,
she is inspirational,
she has a heart of gold,
gosh, I really wish she was here,
I want her so much.

Damaris Asuquo (11)
St Vincent's Primary School, Carnwadric

The Hidden Door

One day, me and my friends were playing hide-and-seek outside,
We didn't have to hide outside, you could have hidden inside,
You are probably wondering who my friends are,
I will tell you later in the poem because we were playing on the tar,
When I was hiding, I found this door, I touched it and then I screamed,
I screamed because I saw the Wizard of Oz,
I went in and my friends followed me,
When we went in, at the door, we found a key to set us free,
But before we turned around, the door shut,
We saw a path into the woods,
We went and explored the good woods,
When we were exploring, I fell onto the ground
And all of a sudden, I got a cut,
When I got a cut, I woke up and it was a dream.

Connie Mackain (11)
Strathpeffer Primary School, Strathpeffer

Riding On A Dragon

Sailing to my cool island,
Where I can see a fiery red dragon,
Sitting, relaxing, on a rock,
Around about five o'clock.
I trained Flame to do a flip
And he let me ride in the dip.

Up and down, in and out,
Both of us splashing all about.
Salty water, tangled hair,
Riding the dip like a funfair.
Through the waves, hand in hand,
Falling, tumbling to the sound.

Lots of shouting, tittle-tattle,
And then it starts, the major battle.
Feet and fists, out and in,
Oh the fight, what a din!
I will not surrender,
I will win!

Evie Hallam (11)
Strathpeffer Primary School, Strathpeffer

Lost On An Island

L ost and scared, nowhere to go,
O n a creepy island where no one goes,
S tuck and cold, no one to hold,
T he wind is going through me like a ghost.

O ver my head goes a helicopter, but they don't see me,
N o hope and no help.

A ll hope is lost,
N o, I think it's in my head!

I make for the shore,
S ometime, a boat might come,
L oud and clear
A nd I see no one,
N ow I can go home safe and sound,
D reams can be fun!

Orrin Stirling-Guy (11)
Strathpeffer Primary School, Strathpeffer

It's Alive

I draw a whale at school one day,
T he whale is alive!
S oaking wet and it's moving,

A live in the drawing, moving and soaking wet,
L iving in a drawing, what are the chances?
I t's not climbing out of the drawing,
V ery small as it jumps into my arms,
E xtremely fast, it shoots back into the drawing.

Daniel Hallam (11)
Strathpeffer Primary School, Strathpeffer

Alone At Night

A ll I can see is darkness in my room,
L ying in my bed,
O ut of my window, I see a black cat, staring at me,
N ext, I hear a crash, the cat has gone,
E verything is quiet but I can hear something outside.

A t that moment, there are three, long knocks at the door,
T onight is a full moon!

N othing scares me more than the silence in my house while my parents are in bed,
I t is the scariest night of my life,
G rinning shadows coming through my door,
"H elp!" I try to shout, but no words come out,
"T igger!" It is the cat from next door, creeping into my room.

Ethan James Bennett (8)
Whinhill Primary School, Greenock

Dream Wonderland

I go on an adventure I will remember,
I wake up to see that there is an alicorn
And my mum next to me,
I figure out that I am a fairy
Called Mary Berry.
When I'm in a good mood
I sing about wings,
I also have magical powers!
After five minutes, the alicorn likes me
And becomes my pet and bows down
To eat the clouds
And accidentally hurts Mum.
Then, *poof*, "Oh, hi girls!" says my dad.
"Hi!" we both say.
After a long chat, my mum asks if I am going to heal her,
So I do.
Close to the end, I find a fancy power bracelet and I put it on.
I wake up and see an alicorn plushy and fairy dust!

Lisa Gillen (8)
Whinhill Primary School, Greenock

Superpowers

S uperpowers, I have many,
U tterly powerful, here comes Princess Penny,
P rincess Penny has a dragon, flying high, people screaming,
E veryone shouting, eek is this a dream?
R unning and screaming, the people go,
P rincess Dragon is here, oh no!
O h wait, the dragon is nice, but he's hurt and falling,
W hoosh! Bang! "Alakazam!" I shout and point at the skies,
E veryone gasps, worry in their eyes,
R ed flashes fill the land, the Princess's Dragon is safe, hip hip hooray,
S he lands safe and well, everyone claps, my superpowers saved the day!

Emily Ruth Humphreys (9)
Whinhill Primary School, Greenock

The Clown Chase

T onight was a horrifying night,
H elp, oh help! Me and my friends ran away screaming,
E very step we took was like a beat of our heart,

C runch! I stood on a big twig,
L ooking around, we saw an abandoned barn,
O wls hooted as we ran towards it,
"W hat's happening?" Brooke exclaimed.
N o one could answer.

C reepy clowns surrounded us,
H olding black and red horns that sounded like children screaming,
A plan struck me like lightning,
S o, we climbed a ladder and an open door,
E scape! The clowns couldn't follow us now!

Eilidh MacNab (8)
Whinhill Primary School, Greenock

Fairy Land

Once upon a dream,
My alicorn and I fly into the night,
We fly higher and higher, out of sight,
Deeper and deeper into the stars,
I can see the magic tunnel
Just past Mars,
In the tunnel now, too dark to see,
Can only feel the butterflies in my tummy,
I try not to feel scared while hugging my alicorn,
I feel the glitter landing in my hair
And realise it's fairy dust flowing through the air,
I can feel my wings pop out and flutter
And know I am a fairy
And can fly alongside my alicorn, Berry Butter.

Brooke Dickson (8)
Whinhill Primary School, Greenock

Royalty Dancer

Rivers rushing, trees brushing,
O ver the wall, there's a castle,
Y oung Anastasia is asleep,
A sleep, not a peep,
L iterally, as she wakes,
T imone, the tiger, tickles her
Y oung Anastasia leaves the castle,

D ancing all about,
A nja, the queen, thinks she's asleep,
N ot a doubt about it,
C an she make it back in time?
E very night she does this,
R uns away and back again.

Taylor Dickson (8)
Whinhill Primary School, Greenock

Superpowers

One day, I woke up to having superpowers,
I felt magic, like I could do anything,
I was in a superhero base
And there were going to be superhero suits,
I could see a beam of light,
I went to see it
And I touched the crystal
And I got my superpowers and a suit,
I was sent on a mission to defeat the bad guys
With my superpowers
And that made me feel amazing and excited
Because everyone relied on me
To make the bad guys go away
And that's exactly what I did!

Ethan McIntosh (8)
Whinhill Primary School, Greenock

Unicorn Nightmares

The evil unicorn came running at me,
In the dark, wet woods where I stood, alone,
Thunder and lightning came crashing down,
I was terrified,
I had no escape,
I hid behind the branches on the trees which were crashing down with the force of the lightning,
Suddenly, something hit my head,
The evil unicorn launched a branch at my head,
Instantly, I dropped to the wet, crunchy grass,
I was about to be caught,
"Wake up Ava! Wake up!"
Thank goodness it was all a dream!

Ava Young (8)
Whinhill Primary School, Greenock

In The Middle Of The Clouds

When I dreamt at night,
In my dream, I saw a light,
I got a bit of a fright,
It was such an awesome sight.

In the light, I saw a unicorn and a fairy,
Holding a bright red berry, yum-yum!
They were flying in the rainbow sky,
Towards the faraway lands, oh my!

Everything was soft and fluffy,
In the middle of the clouds, it was puffy,
The fairy and the unicorn flew away,
Then I woke up and had a great day!

Abigail Eva Milligan (8)
Whinhill Primary School, Greenock

The Dragon

I once had a dream
About a lonely dragon called Bill,
Who was so angry
He would eat, fly and kill,
He loved to set things on fire,
Including the woods
And the shire
And the old grain mill,
His eyes were gold,
His scales were blue,
He's bigger than me
And bigger than you,
We now have a happy dragon,
That dragon called Bill,
He now lives in his cave
With his dragon friend, called Jill!

Kyle Duncan Thompson (8)
Whinhill Primary School, Greenock

A Millionaire

One day, I woke up a millionaire,
Was it a dream? I didn't care,
I could buy a big, big house
Or perhaps buy a magical mouse.

I couldn't believe what I saw,
A drawing of me, looking like a famous rockstar,
I spent some money on a llama
But that just caused a lot of drama.

I went home to my mum,
Today was a lot of fun,
I hope it will happen on another day.

Olivia Logsdon (9)
Whinhill Primary School, Greenock

Fright Night

F riday night, the ghosts all fight,
R ight in the street,
I really hope not to meet a
G host,
H igh the ghosts fly,
T hey look down from up high.

N ight is almost over,
I n my house, I feel safe,
G hosts are now gone, flown up the stream,
H igh in the sky,
T his was all in my dream.

Mia Gorman (8)
Whinhill Primary School, Greenock

Dragon Tsunami

D ragons flying through the air,
R apidly racing to get somewhere,
A ll through the clouds, way up high,
G one in seconds in the sky,
O thers spotted from down below,
N otice a volcano starting to blow,
S parks and ashes lighting the way, oh no! A dragon tsunami!

Cameron Kelly (8)
Whinhill Primary School, Greenock

Alone At Night

I close my eyes, suddenly there's light,
I'm a cowboy, a pirate, a spaceman in flight,
I travel the world across land, sea and sky,
The funny thing is, it seems I can fly,
I've fought Captain Blackbeard and landed on the moon,
Darn it, my alarm clock went off too soon!

Lochlainn Dale (8)
Whinhill Primary School, Greenock

I Wish I Could Fly

I lie on the beach, looking up to the sun,
Sand in my toes, I am having fun,
The clouds look like fluffy pillows up in the sky,
The birds flying high, I wish I could fly,
I shut my eyes and started to dream,
I missed the van that sold ice cream!

Nicholas Robertson (8)
Whinhill Primary School, Greenock

I See A Unicorn

U nbelievably beautiful,
N ational animal of Scotland,
I ridescent in colour,
C ourageous and tall,
O bviously intelligent,
R ock star of all animals,
N ever existed? I don't think so!

Paige Louisa McLennan (8)
Whinhill Primary School, Greenock

Est.1991

YOUNG WRITERS INFORMATION

We hope you have enjoyed reading this book – and that you will continue to in the coming years.

If you're a young writer who enjoys reading and creative writing, or the parent of an enthusiastic poet or story writer, do visit our website **www.youngwriters.co.uk**. Here you will find free competitions, workshops and games, as well as recommended reads, a poetry glossary and our blog.

If you would like to order further copies of this book, or any of our other titles, then please give us a call or visit **www.youngwriters.co.uk**.

Young Writers
Remus House
Coltsfoot Drive
Peterborough
PE2 9BF
(01733) 890066
info@youngwriters.co.uk